Table of Contents

Introduction

Mushrooms are a staple of a variety of different culinary traditions and one of the few fungi that we are happy to see when we look inside our refrigerators. Although historically humans have consumed a diverse array of mushrooms for nutritional and medicinal purposes, it is only in recent years that this diversity has been brought to the foreground of culinary practice.As commercial cultivation improves, and global markets expand, the variety of readily accessible mushrooms has increased substantially. This can be daunting for the novice mushroom consumer, who is faced with a staggering number of foreign fungi to wade through. When approached with an adventurous spirit, mushrooms can be an exciting, and delicious exploration of a veritable garden of earthly delights. "Oyster Mushroom," is the quintessential pleurotoid mushroom: it is a gilled mushroom with a very short stalk that fruits from the sides of logs. Oyster Mushrooms are some of the best edible wild mushrooms; they are fairly easy to identify, they are meaty, and they appear in large numbers. Additionally, you find them in late fall and winter, when the woods are otherwise boring places for mushroom hunters. Although it grows on hardwood logs in nature. Ostreatus will decompose pretty much any plant material, which makes it very easy to cultivate. As an added bonus, the Oyster Mushroom attacks nematodes.

What Are Oyster Mushrooms

Oyster mushrooms are beloved the world over for their delicate texture and mild, savory flavor. The mushrooms typically have broad, thin, oyster- or fan-shaped caps and are white, gray, or tan, with gills lining the underside. The caps are sometimes frilly-edged and can be found in clusters of small mushrooms or individually as larger mushrooms. Oyster mushrooms are more expensive than white button mushrooms but less so than rarer mushrooms like morels, and take little prep since they can be used whole or chopped. They are even used to make mycelium furniture and many other products.

History

The oyster mushroom grows in temperate and deciduous forests around the world, except for the Pacific Northwest of North America, living on the wood of decomposing deciduous trees.Because it is so often found on the trunks of dead and decaying trees, particularly beech trees, some early biologists believed it to be a parasite.However, it is in fact a saprophytic organism, living on the bacteria and nematodes that thrive in decaying wood, growing on trees that are dying from other causes.Oyster mushrooms were first documented in 1775, by Dutch naturalist Nikolaus Joseph Freiherr von Jacquin. They were first cultivated as a food source in Germany during WWI, and developed into a commercial food product in the early 1940s in response to war-time food shortages. Since the 1940s, commercial cultivation of the oyster mushroom has spread around the world. In East Asian cuisines, it is considered a delicacy, and in parts of Asia and Europe it is prepared and served much like meat in traditional dishes. It was firstly sophisticated in Germany during the World War I.It is grown economically in the world as a food. It is cultivated as similar to the king Oyster mushroom.These mushrooms are also used for industrial purposes.These fungi are cultivated worldwide generally in the India, South East Asia, Africa and Europe. In the 18th century, Joseph Freiherr von Jacquin assigned the Oyster mushrooms in the Agarius family due to the presence of gills underneath the cap.In 1871, Paul Kummar, a German mucologist assigned the mushroom in Pleurotus family. Germany grew Oyster mushroom during World War I as a necessity food which discovered the antibiotic qualities of this mushroom.

Types of Oyster Mushroom

- Blue Oyster (Pleurotus ostreatus var. columbinus)
- Highlights: Good for cooler temperatures, fast growing
- Lowlights: Needs TONS of fresh air for normal looking fruits

The Blue Oyster mushroom is a good choice for new growers, and is perfectly suitable for cooler temperatures.In fact, the colder the temperature during fruiting, the more distinctly blue this mushroom appears. Either way, the blue is most noticeable in the early stages of growth- but turns to grey as the mushroom matures.

Yellow Oyster (Pleurotus citrinopileatus)

Highlights: Beautiful yellow color through entire growth cycle, fast growing, high CO2 tolerant

Lowlights: Delicate fruits, shorter shelf life, so-so flavour

The Yellow Oyster is a real head turner.

It produces beautiful but delicate "bouquets" of thin capped yellow mushrooms.They also smell distinctly like citrous fruit when fresh. The yellow oyster is fast to fruit and easy to grow, being much more tolerant of low fresh air intake than many other types of Oyster. Unfortunately, the yellow color is lost during cooking, and the flavor of yellow oysters is nothing to write home about. Further, yellow oysters have a terrible shelf life, only lasting a few days in the fridge before starting to smell a little like urine. That is likely why they aren't common at the grocery store- and are better enjoyed as fresh as possible. Although the Yellow Oyster can grow on a wide variety of substrates, I have never had good luck when trying to grow it on straw. It seems to do much better on hardwood sawdust amended with bran, or with the masters mix.

Pink Oyster (Pleurotus djamor)

Highlights: Striking pink color, nice thick fruits, easy to grow on straw, heat tolerant

Lowlights: Short shelf life, can die in cooler temperatures

- Much like its Yellow cousin, the Pink Oyster is strikingly distinct and beautiful. The vibrantly pink mushrooms burst off the substrate in huge floral bouquets, and are a favorite among passers by at the farmers market.

- The fruits are usually large, and no where near as delicate as the Yellows.
- Pink Oysters are also famously heat tolerant. They are suitable to be grown in places where grow room temperatures exceed 30 deg C. Cold temperatures can easily kill the mycelium of Pink Oysters, making it a difficult species for storing spawn or cultures in the fridge. That being said, the shelf life for Pink Oysters is extremely stunted. After harvest, they'll last but a few days in the fridge before no longer being viable for consumption. Because of this, they need to be sold almost immediately after harvest- a difficult challenge for many small growers

Elm Oyster (Hypsizygus ulmarius)

Highlights: Well adapted to high CO_2, high yield, low spore load

Lowlights: No striking color, short shelf life

- The Elm Oyster is not a "true" oyster in that it is not in the "Pleurotus" family, although it is a closely related cousin, and most growers still refer to it as an Oyster.

That being said, it does have a few advantages over most other Oysters that make it worth your consideration.

- The Elm Oyster is much better at forming normal looking fruits in high CO2 environments, which makes it an excellent candidate for indoor growers, or grow rooms that have a hard time managing the high fresh air requirements of other Oysters. It also has a much lower "spore load" than most other Oysters, which can save lots of clean-up and clogged fans.
- The Elm Oyster is typically white-beige in color, and forms nice large caps in dense clusters. It grows well on hardwood sawdust or the masters mix. It is fast to colonize, and very friendly to beginners.

Pearl Oyster (Pleurotus ostreatus)

Highlights: Easily available, easy to grow, decent shelf life, good in cooking, grows on many substrates

Lowlights: High fresh air requirement

- This is the "standard" archetypal Oyster mushroom, widely grown all over the world. Pearl Oysters grow fast, and fruit heavily- often achieving biological efficiency of over 100%.

- They can grow on a variety of substrates, including hardwood sawdust, hardwood chips, wheat straw, oat straw, grass clippings, coco-coir, and almost any other linginous material. The shelf life for Pearl Oysters is decent- better than Pinks or Yellows, but not as good as Kings.

- Aside from the fresh air requirement, Pearl Oysters are an easy entry to growing for new growers, and because of that, they are quite popular in mushroom growing kits like the super popular Back to The Roots mushroom growing kit.

Phoenix Oyster (Pleurotus pulminarious)

Highlights: Good for warm weather, fast growing, widely grown, good yield

Lowlights: Short shelf life, high spore load, in-vitro pinning

- The Pheonix Oyster, also known as the Lung Oyster, Indian Oyster, or the Italian Oyster, is very similar to the standard Pearl Oyster mushroom. The major difference is that Phoenix Oysters can withstand warmer temperatures than Pearl Oyster. In nature, they typically fruit much later in the summer.

- They will also have smaller, thinner caps and a slightly different color. Still, Phoenix Oysters are a very popular cultivar for all types of growers.

King Oyster (Pleurotus eryngii)

Highlights: Best shelf life, versatile, meaty texture

Lowlights: Susceptible to bacterial blotch

- Most Oyster species will grow in large clusters, forming multiple shelf-like fruit bodies, all folding over one another.
- King Oysters are distinct, in that they typically grow singly instead of in clusters. Depending on growing conditions, they can sometimes resemble a button mushroom.
- Commercially, King Oysters are often grown in high CO2, low light conditions, which causes the mushrooms to form huge fat stems and tiny caps. Unlike many other Oysters, the stems of King Oysters have great texture and flavour, and are often purposely grown to maximize stem size.

- If grown in low CO2, well-lit conditions, they will form large, dark caps- somewhat resembling a portobello.

- Due to the thick, meaty texture, King Oysters have the longest shelf life of any Oyster species. They can sometimes last in the fridge for up to two weeks, making it much easier for smaller growers to manage production schedules to match market days.

- King Oysters will grow on straw, but they are most often grown on sawdust to get a better yield and better quality fruit. A common method of growing King Oysters is to apply a casing layer and "top-fruit" the block.

- Managing the humidity for this species can be finicky, and many growers run into issues with bacterial blotch. Hobby growers are not likely to run into this issue.

Golden Oyster Mushroom (Pleurotus citrinopileatus)

(Golden Oyster Mushroom)Golden oyster mushroom has distinct taste with delightful light yellow color. This mushroom is hypersensitive and low in productivity rate.

Pleurotus cornucopiae

The cap is cream colored during young and turns into yellowish to ochraceous when matured.The cap is funnel shaped with white inner flesh is white and mild taste.

Pleurotus eryngii (King Oyster Mushroom)

It is easy to grow and has a therapeutical utility, less productive in comparison other types of Oyster mushrooms.In addition,It promotes the nutritive supplements same as rye grains or wheat.

(Oyster Mushroom)

Pleurotus ostreatusIt was originated from the Greek word pleura which means side and otus which means ear. It is simple to be grown and various productive strains are found.It could be cultivated in any season. It progress well in low temperatures or high temperatures.

The Florida Oyster Mushroom (Pleurotus florida)

This mushroom was originated from Florida. It is suitable to be grown in moist and warm weather.It is used traditionally all around the world.

Indian Oyster or Phoenix Mushroom (Pleurotus pulmonarius)

This mushroom has the shape and color of human lungs.It consists of varieties such as var. lapponicus, var. juglandis and var. pulmonarius. Juglandis are found on Juglans spp. Trees whereas other grow on the hardwoods as well as conifers beyond subtropical and temperate areas.

Recipes To Cook Those Oyster Mushrooms

These mushrooms are loaded with nutrition such as vitamins and minerals. Here are some of the recipes that helps to understand about the preparation of Oyster mushrooms.

Short And Simple, The Mushroom Soup

It is one of the best methods to use mushrooms in a soup.The mushrooms should be boiled and mixed in a mixer. The oil should be added to the pan and include the ingredients. Add butter as well as salt on a soup. The veggies could be added to make it more healthy.

Quick And Easy Tacos

It is a simple way to use Oysters.Take a pack of tacos and few vegetables with oyster mushrooms such as carrots, cheese, bell peppers and broccoli. Cut all the veggies into small pieces. Add little butter in a pan and then sauté vegetables. Then add pepper and salt the vegetables for a taste.Let it become cool.Now take tacos and add the mix on taco.Then serve.

How To Use Oyster Mushrooms

Oyster mushrooms could be added to stir fry or sauté in the olive oil and garlic.It is a best replacement for portobello and button mushrooms. Oyster mushrooms enhance the taste of soups and sauces. The supplements of Oyster mushroom could be found in the form of supplements.It could be taken in capsule form.It provides the same effect on cholesterol and also enhances an immune system.Two capsules in a day provides 200 mg of Oyster mushroom, when it is taken along with full glass of water or meal.

Facts About Oyster Mushroom

Medicinal Oysters: Cancer and Cholesterol

- In addition to helping the environment, oyster mushrooms can help your body as well! So far they seem to have the most promising effect on cholesterol levels and cancer.
- Oyster mushrooms Oysters naturally produce compounds called statins. Statin drugs reduce "bad

cholesterol" (LDL) by stimulating receptors in the liver to clear the cholesterol from the body.

- Studies have shown a link between consuming Pleurotus ostreatus and a lowering of cholesterol levels, no doubt due to the statins they produce. Hopefully future research will reveal exactly how much to eat to get these effects.

- As for cancer, research shows a possible anti-tumor effect from polysaccharides in oysters. A polysaccharide is a complex carbohydrate made up of smaller sugar molecules.

- Specific polysaccharides, known as beta-D-glucans, are suspected to stimulate the immune system to fight cancer.The beta-D-glucan isolated from oyster mushrooms is called pleuran.

- Studies are ongoing into the effects of pleuran for cancer treatment. Eventually I'd like to link to a legitimate human trial, as all those i've found so far have used laboratory animals.

- Oyster mushrooms are also a popular edible. They have a nutty, subtle flavor that goes well in soups, stews, and sauces.

- Fortunately Pleurotus ostreatus is one of the easiest species to cultivate. If you're not into growing your own mushrooms, you can find them in the woods or your local grocery store (where you may see wildlife of a different sort).

- If you do plan on finding them in the forest be sure to look on hardwoods (oak, maple, aspen, elm, etc.) Anytime from spring to fall. Don't forget to look up as well. I've found them fruiting in a vertical line high up trees as well as at eye level. As always, be sure you know what you've picked or double check with someone who does.

- Oysters are commonly home to beetles and other bugs so they'll need to be wiped and cleaned once you bring them home. They dry and reconstitute very well so don't hesitate to dry them and save some for later!

- Use caution if trying them for the first time. Some people are allergic to their spores while others may experience an upset stomach. Try a small amount first to see how your body reacts.

- Although they go well in many dishes, the most common way to cook oysters is a simple sautee or stir fry. Brown them in olive oil with herbs and spices of your choice.

Enjoy

Health Benefits Of Oyster Mushroom

High Cholesterol

A preliminary study published in Journal of Physiology and Biochemistry in 2013 found that oyster mushrooms may reduce cholesterol levels.In tests on rats, the study's authors observed that treatment for seven days with an oral oyster mushroom extract helped increase the animals' antioxidant status and decreased their levels of cholesterol and triglycerides. High triglyceride levels have been associated with an increased risk of cardiovascular disease.

Immune Function

Oyster mushrooms may enhance immune function, according to a small study published in the Journal of Traditional and Complementary Medicine in 2015. For the study, participants ingested an oyster mushroom extract for eight weeks. At the study's end, researchers found evidence that the extract may have immune-enhancing effects.

Cancer

Some preliminary research indicates that oyster mushrooms may possess cancer-fighting properties. This research includes a study published in International Journal of Oncology in 2008, in which tests on human cells demonstrated that an oyster mushroom extract may suppress the growth and spread of breast cancer and colon cancer. Additionally, a mouse-based study published in the International Journal of Medicinal Mushrooms in 2011 determined that an oyster mushroom extract may fight tumor growth, in part by activating certain immune cells.Oyster mushrooms are mostly found in the Chinese foods. Due to its high amount of nutrients, it is widely popular.Oyster mushroom is sautéed with garlic and olive oil. They are loaded with various amounts of nutrients and vitamins which makes them a healthy diet. It is free from fat, cholesterol, gluten, low in calories and sodium.The iron found in Oyster mushrooms is high in comparison to the meat.

Maintain The Levels Of Blood Sugar

The insufficient amount of insulin in the body results in diabetes.The calcium is required for the insulin secretion. Vitamin D helps to reduce inflammation and raise the insulin sensitivity.The studies shows that Vitamin D helps to prevent both type 1 and type 2 diabetes.

Immunity System

Vitamin D helps to replicate the healthy cells and protects the autoimmune conditions such as flu and common cold. It also prevents the excessive or prolonged inflammatory responses. Inflammation is the cause for autoimmune disorders and chronic diseases such as rheumatoid arthritis, multiple sclerosis, irritable bowel syndrome, high blood pressure and digestive problems.

Cardiovascular Conditions

Besides the balance of triglycerides and cholesterol levels, Vitamin B3 helps to reduce atherosclerosis that is hardening of arteries which may lead to the heart disease.It also assists to reduce the histamine production and inflammation along with the improvement in circulation. Vitamin B3 reduces the chances of reoccurring of heart disease or cardiac arrest in those who have already experienced. Additionally, Vitamin B3 helps to treat pellagra which is the health condition that occurs from the deficiency of niacin.

Skin problems

Vitamin B3 which is in the form of niacinamide helps to clear acne when it is applied topically in the skin. Niacin assists in the reduction of flare ups, skin inflammation, redness and irritation. It also helps to treat granuloma annulare and bullous pemphigoid which is a skin disease that blisters the skin, cause pain and infection.

Brain Health

The studies show that copper has an impact on the brain pathways such as galactose and dopamine which helps to maintain the energy, mood, focus and outlook.The deficiency of copper results in fatigue, low metabolic activity, poor mood and problem in concentration. Copper also helps to utilize the antioxidants such as superoxide dismutase, Vitamin C, tyrosinase and ascorbate oxidase. This helps to prevent the damage made by free radicals in the brain and also slows down the process of ageing, neuro-degenerative diseases and cancer.

Cures Anemia

An inadequate amount of oxygen in the blood, low red bloods cell production and the blood loss are the causes of Anemia. Vitamin B2 helps to prevent the anemia.Vitamin B2 is vital for production of red blood cells and steroid hormone synthesis. It assists in transporting the oxygen in the body and also mobilizes iron. The people with low Vitamin B2 have the high chances of sickle cell anemia and anemia. The research shows that Vitamin B2 helps to reduce the homocysteine levels in the blood.

Provides Energy

Vitamin B converts the carbohydrate into glucose which is used as a fuel to produce energy. Vitamin B synthesizes the body and metabolizes proteins and fats.Vitamin B5 assist to rebuild muscles, tissues and organs. Vitamin B5 helps to maintain the optimum level of metabolism.

Prevents Tooth Decay

Vitamin D, phosphorus and calcium helps to form and maintain the dental health by assisting the jaw-bone mineral density, holding the teeth and tooth enamel.Children need calcium and phosphorus rich foods to develop the adult teeth and form the hard structure of teeth. Vitamin D requires phosphorus to balance the calcium and enhance absorption while forming tooth. Vitamin D reduces the gum inflammation which is related to periodontal gum disease.

Maintains Mood

Neurotransmitter functions depend on the adequate amount of iron to maintain a positive mood. It also depends on the hormone balance such as dopamine, serotonin and others. So the deficiency of iron leads to bad sleep, poor mood, lack of motivation and low level of energy.

Alcoholism

Vitamin B1 assist to reduce the chances of brain disorder named as Wernicke-Korsakoff Syndrome which includes nerve damage, muscle movement, problem in walking and lethargy.It is caused due to the low thiamine and poor diet but is usually seen in the alcoholics. The high intake of thiamine can reduce the symptoms of alcohol

Disadvantages

- Not all interested individuals can be given the opportunity to engage in mushroom production because of some limitations in economically obtainable sources of bedding materials.
- The quality of the produce is rather hard to maintain due to varying conditions of growth in different mushroom communities.
- The type of management varies from place to place because problems obtaining in one mushroomgrowing community are not necessarily the same in others, hence a case-to-case basis is needed for problem-solving.
- Owing to several factors affecting production, the target yield is not usually attained. This is primarily because of lack of sufficient experience by the farmers. An unstable volume of production has an adverse effect on the marketing system.
- Oyster mushroom contains a HMG-CoA reductase enzyme inhibitor substance called stating (lovastatin or Mevinolin-2.8% dry weight).

Basic Steps To Growing Oyster Mushrooms

Inoculation

The first step in inoculation, where you add mushroom grain spawn (think of it like seeds) to a suitable substrate (think of it like soil). Grain spawn can either be made at home, or bought pre-made. You'll want to add the spawn at a rate of about 10%. That means if you have 20 lbs of substrate (like wet straw) you'll want to add about 2 lbs of spawn. The spawn needs to be mixed thoroughly in order to get the most possible "inoculation points".

Colonization (Incubatinon)

Once the spawn is added to the substrate, it will start to expand and grow over it's new territory, spreading out and devouring nutrients. This process is known as "colonization". After a couple weeks, the mycelium will have completly engulfed the new substrate and is said to be "fully colonized"

Fruiting

Once the substrate is fully colonized, it will continue to get thicker until it is fully consolidated. Eventually, little pins will start to form.

Soil Types For Growing Mushrooms

Mushroom growing is a unique type of gardening.Mushrooms are really the fruit of a fungus that is grown from spores, or "mycelium," a mat of developing spores.Mycelium is also called mushroom "spawn." Ordinary soil does not provide the right kind of nutrients for growing mushrooms.Instead, other materials such as straw, sawdust, wood chips and compost are used as growing medium, called a "substrate."Different types of mushrooms require different kinds of substrate.

Wood Chips

According to the University of California at Davis, wood chips can be used as the soil medium for those mushrooms that grow well on wood substrates.Mushrooms that grow in woody materials include oyster, shiitake, reishi, maitake and lion's mane mushrooms.You can purchase pre-sterilized wood chips ready for culturing the mushroom spawn.

Compost

Compost is a substrate that requires the most time to prepare, but it makes an effective soil-substitute for growing mushrooms.Compost is a mixture of yard waste, like leaves, grass clippings, weeds and branches, with kitchen waste like coffee grounds, vegetable scraps, eggshells and shells. This matter is kept moist and warm until it deteriorates into a rich, loamy soil-like material. You can make your own compost in a small enclosure in your yard in two to four months, according to the Pennsylvania Department of Environmental Protection. White button mushrooms prefer compost as substrate.

Straw

Straw can also be use as the substrate soil-substitute for growing mushrooms. According to Shroomery, cut wheat or barley straw into 2 to 4 inch pieces and pasteurized by putting it into 150-degree F water for 1 hour, then removed and allowed to drain. It is then cooled to room temperature. It is then placed in a bag with the mushroom mycelium, punctured several times and allowed to grow. Once the mycelium spreads on the surface, the bag is opened and the mushrooms are exposed to the air.

Horse Manure

Horse manure grows mushrooms easily if composted well and mixed with straw. You can then place the mushroom spawn on the surface of the manure compost and rub it into the surface.A bit of lime will help the mushrooms grow. Do not water the manure compost for four weeks, as there is sufficient moisture in the compost, according to CountryFarm Lifestyle.You can purchase sterilized and composted horse manure for your mushroom substrate.

Potting Soil

You can also use ordinary potting soil to grow mushrooms, but you must add additional organic material for the mushroom spawn to eat. Coffee beans, cut in half and soaked in water for five minutes, then placed on the soil gives the potting soil more structure and nutrients for growing mushrooms. Adding vermiculite will give the soil additional body to hold the spawn.

Cultivation

Oyster mushroom is unique in being the only edible saphrophytic fungus preys on certain nematodes and insects from which it gets nitrogen to flourish. In their natural habitat, pleurotus species grow on dead and decaying logs, living tree trunks of coniferous and beech trees.Oyster mushroom cultivation under supervised farms has revolutionized its continuous supply to the ever increasing consumer demands.Any kind of sawdust and agriculture-waste that is rich in lignin and cellulose can become suitable substrate fro its cultivation. Fruit bodies appear about 25 days after spawn inoculation.

Selection And Storage

Fresh and dried oyster mushrooms can be readily available in the US supermarkets. Choose non slimy and evenly colored oyster mushrooms, with a smooth cap and no black spots. Pleurotus mushrooms are highly perishable and absorb the flavor of surrounding foods. Consume them immediately.They also sold dried, and in brine in these stores. For storage, place them in a paper bag or in a dish covered with cloth for a short period (2-3 days). Dried oyster in sealed packs and vacuum packs can stay well for many months.

Preparation And Serving Methods

Fresh oyster mushrooms do not require washing.Just clean any surface dirt or sand particle using a soft brush. You can tear the ears (caps) by hand since they cook evenly in the dishes because the uniform thickness of caps. Oyster mushrooms impart mild mushroomy flavor, and distinct fleshy texture in the dishes. Thus, they can be an ideal substitute in the dishes that call for pork or poultry. Do not mask their flavor by pairing them with strongly flavored foods or cooking them in large amount of butter or oil. They can be sautéed or boiled 3-5 min, quick braised or baked for 7-10 min.Their stems require a longer cooking time and benefit from being chopped evenly.

Oyster Mushroom Recipes

One of the most popular ways to cook oyster mushrooms is to stir-fry or sauté them.This requires a preheated hot pan, a small amount of liquid, and stirring.Make sure to give them space so their moisture can cook off, that way they will truly sauté rather than steam. Serve as a side dish or use in sauces, stir-fries, pastas, risotto, or even to top toast. Because they get so silky when cooked, oyster mushrooms respond well to braising, too. Add them to soups and stews or sauces. The mushrooms can also be grilled whole on skewers, roasted, or dredged in a crispy coating and deep-fried.

Vegan Mushroom Cream Sauce For Pasta

Enjoy the taste of a deliciously creamy vegan mushroom sauce. Instead of cream, this dairy-free recipe uses vegan margarine and soy milk, and it's easy to make from scratch.Fresh chopped parsley, garlic, and a touch of freshly cracked black pepper give it an Italian-inspired flavor that's perfect for fettuccine or linguine pasta. You can also pour it over egg noodles, baked potatoes, or any type of mock meat, including tofu steaks. Make this sauce with any variety of mushrooms you like.Try button, oyster, portobello, or shiitake mushrooms, or create a custom combination of mushrooms. There are also many ways you can adapt it for other meals. For instance, you can skip the mushrooms for a dairy-free white sauce, switch out the herbs, or add veggies.

Ingredients

- 2 tablespoons vegan margarine (divided)
- 8–12 ounces mushrooms (sliced)
- 1 clove garlic (minced)
- 1 tablespoon flour
- 1 1/4 cups soy milk (unsweetened)
- 1 tablespoon parsley (fresh; chopped, plus more for garnish)
- 1/2 lemon (juiced; about 1 to 1 1/2 tablespoons)
- Pinch of salt (sea or Kosher; to taste)
- Pinch of black pepper (freshly ground; to taste)
- 10 ounces pasta (cooked according to package instructions)

Steps To Make It

- Gather the ingredients.

- Melt 1 tablespoon of the vegan margarine in a saucepan over medium heat. Add the mushrooms and garlic and sauté until soft, about 4 to 5 minutes. Remove the mushrooms and garlic from the pan and set aside.

- Again over medium heat, melt the second tablespoon of vegan margarine. Stir in the flour to form a paste and allow to cook for about 1 minute.

- Gradually stir in the soy milk and whisk the mixture together until it's smooth and a thick paste.

- Add the mushrooms, fresh parsley, lemon juice, salt, and pepper. Cook for 1 to 2 minutes, or until thick.

- Pour the fresh mushroom cream sauce over warm cooked pasta or noodles, garnish with fresh chopped parsley (if desired), and serve immediately.

Enjoy

Tips

When finishing the sauce, there are a couple of things you can do if it doesn't get as thick as you like. The first step to try is to simply turn up the heat. Stir it regularly and watch it so the sauce doesn't scorch. You can also stir in a bit more flour or even corn starch 1 tablespoon of either should do to get it to thicken up.

Fried Mushrooms

Fried mushrooms are crispy on the outside, tender and juicy on the inside.It is remarkable how frying turns mushrooms into a fun snack or appetizer.Both wild or cultivated mushroom varieties work equally well in this recipe. Be sure to clean wild morels thoroughly since their sponge-like texture tends to hold plenty of what we'll politely call grit from the forest floor. You may want to cut larger mushrooms into one-bite pieces, but that's a matter of taste. Whereas most fried mushroom recipes use a batter to coat the fungi, this recipe keeps things simple and ultra-easy with a quick dip in buttermilk and then a light dredge in seasoned flour, just like the best-fried chicken. This is as much a method as it is a recipe, so feel free to make larger or smaller batches as befits your audience.

Ingredients

- 1 pound mushrooms
- 1/2 cup buttermilk
- 1 cup flour
- 1 teaspoon fine sea salt (plus more for sprinkling)

- Oil (peanut, vegetable, grapeseed, or canola oil, for frying)

Steps To Make It

- Gather the ingredients.

- Trim, rinse, and thoroughly dry the mushrooms. Cut into pieces if desired.

- Put the mushrooms in a medium bowl, pour the buttermilk over them, and toss them with the buttermilk to coat. Set aside.

- Bring about 1/2 inch of oil in a wide, heavy pot to 350 F to 375 F over high heat. Adjust the heat to maintain that temperature range. It's best to test the temperature by using a thermometer, but dipping the handle of a wooden spoon into the oil works too. If the oil immediately bubbles around the handle, it is hot enough to fry the mushrooms; if it doesn't bubble right away, it's not hot enough; if it bubbles quickly and violently, the oil is too hot.

- While the oil heats, combine the flour and salt in a large bowl or re-sealable plastic bag.

- Drain the mushrooms or lift them out of the buttermilk. Toss them gently in the flour mixture to coat them thoroughly.

- Shake any excess flour off the mushrooms as you lift them out of the flour.

- Add enough mushrooms to the oil to form a single layer. The single-layer bit is key: if the mushrooms are too crowded and not free to bob around in the hot oil a bit, instead of cooking evenly and turning golden and crunchy, bits will remain soggy and get oily.

- Fry until golden brown and the mushrooms are Transfer mushrooms to paper toweltender all the way through— about 3 minutes.

- Transfer the mushrooms with tongs or a slotted spoon to a cooling rack set over paper towels and sprinkle with more salt (if you're a salt lover, consider using big crystals of crunchy sea salt at this point) and serve hot.

- Transfer mushrooms to paper towel

- Repeat with remaining mushrooms only cooking as many as can fit in a single layer in the oil at a time.

- You can serve your mushrooms with the dip or condiment of your choice. A horseradish dip or chipotle dip goes well with mushrooms.

- Serve fried mushrooms

Enjoy

Stir-Fry Up A Delicious Dish Of Shrimp With Chinese Greens

Marinated shrimp are combined with Chinese greens (bok choy) and mushrooms in this simple stir-fry recipe with a light sauce that lets the natural flavor of the ingredients shine. It's an easy dish that takes about 6 minutes to cook and about 20 minutes to prep. That means you can have a delicious meal on the table in less than 30 minutes. This makes a complete meal for two when served with rice or when served as a multi-course meal, it easily can feed up to four.

Ingredients

- 1/2 to 3/4 pound shrimp (peeled and deveined)
- 1 tablespoon Chinese rice wine (or dry sherry)
- 1/2 teaspoon salt
- 1 tablespoon cornstarch
- 1/2 pound Chinese greens (bok choy)
- 4 ounces fresh mushrooms (or 6 Chinese dried mushrooms or dried shiitake mushrooms)

- 2 tablespoons vegetable oil (or peanut oil for stir-frying, more as needed)

- 2 thin slices ginger (peeled)

- 1/4 teaspoon salt

- 1/4 cup sodium-reduced chicken broth

- 1/2 teaspoon sugar

- 1 tablespoon light soy sauce

Black Pepper (To Taste)

- 1 teaspoon cornstarch (mixed with 2 teaspoons water)

Steps To Make It

- Gather the ingredients.

- If using frozen shrimp, defrost in the refrigerator. Rinse the shrimp under cold running water and pat dry with paper towels

- Place the shrimp in a large bowl and add the rice wine or sherry, 1/2 teaspoon salt, and 1 tablespoon cornstarch, stirring in one direction (this is to make sure the marinade spreads evenly).

- Chop the bok choy stalks diagonally and the leaves across into 1-inch pieces.

- Wipe the mushrooms with a cloth or soft brush and cut into thin slices. If using Chinese dried mushrooms, soak in hot water for 20 minutes to soften. Drain the softened mushrooms, remove the stems, and cut into quarters.

- Heat the wok and add 2 tablespoons oil. When the oil is hot, add the ginger. Stir-fry for about 30 seconds, until aromatic.

- Next, add the shrimp and stir-fry until they turn pink. Remove the cooked shrimp from the pan.

- Add a bit more oil if needed so there are about 1 1/2 tablespoons in the wok. Add the bok choy, mushrooms, and 1/4 teaspoon salt. Stir-fry for 1 minute. If the vegetables seem a bit dry at this point, add a small amount of water or rice wine. Add the chicken broth, cover and cook for 2 more minutes.

- Return the shrimp to the pan. Add the sugar, soy sauce, and pepper.

- Give the cornstarch/water mixture a quick stir and add to the middle of the ingredients, stirring to thicken. Cook, stirring for another minute.

- Serve hot with rice, if desired.

Oyster Mushroom Nutrition

There are numerous studies (source:

Macronutrients

- 48% carbohydrates with 3% total sugars

- 27% crude protein

- 1% crude fat

- 11% crude fibre

- 10% total ash

- Overall protein digestibility is 79%.

Micronutrients

- Iron: 1.33 mg

- Zinc: .77 mg

- Phosphorus: 120 mg

- Manganese: .133 mg

- Calcium: 3 mg

- Potassium: 420 mg

- Magnesium: 18 mg

- Oyster mushrooms are also an excellent source of selenium, but selenium levels depend a great deal on the growth method and substrate of the mushroom. Several studies have been undertaken to boost selenium levels in oyster mushrooms.

- Oyster mushrooms are also very high in vitamin B1, vitamin B2, vitamin B6, vitamin C, vitamin D, thiamin, riboflavin, and niacin.

What all this means is that oyster mushrooms are naturally a great source of

Antioxidants

While most edible mushrooms have high levels of antioxidants, the Pleurotus family, and oyster mushrooms specifically, are higher in antioxidants than other mushroom species.Antioxidants are essential for fighting damage at the cellular level, and are important for boosting physical health, as well as preserving youthful skin.

Polysaccharides

Polysaccharides are special forms of fiber that affect how other nutrients are absorbed by the body. The high levels of polysaccharides in oyster mushrooms help to regulate blood sugar, lower cholesterol, and help to create short-chain fatty acids that are essential for digestive health.

Peptides And Lectins

Peptides and lectins are special proteins.The peptides in oyster mushrooms have beneficial anti-microbial properties, while lectins defend against invading microorganisms.These compounds are believed to be why oyster mushrooms are beneficial to the immune system.

Lovastatin

Statins are the name of a group of chemicals that inhibit the metabolism of cholesterol. Oyster mushrooms have up to 216 mg/kg of lovastatins, which is why they are helpful for regulating cholesterol and improving liver and kidney function.

Ergosterol

Is a precursor to vitamin D production, so it both boosts edible vitamin D in a mushroom, and helps a human naturally synthesize vitamin D from sunlight.

Fatty Acid Esters

The fatty acid esters in oyster mushrooms have anti-bacterial properties, and are used by the body to make healthy dietary fats.

Do Mushrooms Need Sunlight?

Light is not mandatory as it is with plants. Most mushrooms can fruit without light, but they may look strange. Most mushrooms do well with sunlight as long it isn't direct and causing them to dry out. Wild mushrooms have a hard time avoiding all sunlight. Cultivated Agaricus mushrooms (button, crimini, portabella) are grown in the dark as Susan Hadlow describes. These days, after picking, they are often given a pulse of ultraviolet light to cause them to create vitamin D. If they were grown in sunlight, they would produce D on their own. Shiitake and oyster mushrooms, for example, will grow in the dark, but they tend to be white rather than the more familiar brown or gray color.These growers provide plenty of light (sunlight or artificial light) for their mushrooms as they grow.As a result, they have plenty of vitamin D without the extra UV.

Among the diseases observable during the cultivation of Pleurotus eryngii, whatever the growing procedure is, it is yellowing that can cause the most severe damage.The disease is characterized by a yellow discoloration of the pileus and hydropic, often elongated and coalescing areas on the entire stem. Symptomatic basidiomata then stop growing, turn a reddish-brown color and are affected by rotting.Diseased sporophores exhale an odor, which is almost alcohol-like and pleasant at first, but rapidly becomes offensive and nauseating. Pseudomonas agarici and P. reactans are reported as the most likely causal agents of yellowing in both P. eryngii and P. ostreatus (Jacq.) P. Kumm.P. reactans belong to the V group of fluorescent Pseudomonas and is considered to be saprophytic bacteria inhabiting the mushroom hyphosphere.According to Bruno et al. and Kim et al, other bacterial species have been isolated from symptomatic basidiomata (Pseudomonas costantinii, Bacillus cereus, Enterobacter amnigenus, Sphingomonas spp., Staphylococcus epidermidis, Pantoea spp. and Moraxella osloensis). Bessette et al. reported that the yellow blotch in P. ostreatus caused by P. agarici formed a clean yellow fluid on the surface of the cluster at first, and then deformed with an increase in severity. The stipes tended to recurve near the base and the sporocarp was upright. Differences in susceptibility/resistance exhibited by various commercial strains of P. eryngii could play an important role in disease incidence.Yellowing of P. eryngii can occur in all basidioma development phases, from primordia appearance to commercial maturation. Mushroom producers generally try, albeit with disappointing results, to prevent yellowing or halt its development and spread by adding sodium hypochlorite or chemicals containing iodine to irrigation water. Much research has been done to figure out an adequate method to prevent or control this disease. Controls, such as lowering relative air humidity, and watering with low concentration of chlorine solution (calcium chloride and chlorinated compounds) are currently the most commonly utilized chemicals for blotch disease control. When mushrooms remain wet, however, chlorine has little effect since the bacterial population reproduces at a rate that neutralizes the effect of the oxidizing agent.Several other disinfectants and antibiotics, such as chloramine T and bronopol, essential oils, and kasugamycin, have also been tried for their ability to control bacterial blotch disease. According to Bruno et al., it is safe to say that acetic acid at and may be considered an interesting antibacterial tool to prevent and/or halt the yellowing of P. eryngii.

Bacterial Brown Blotch

P. tolaasii is a bacterium, which causes bacterial blotches in the button mushroom Agaricus spp., in Flamulina spp., in oyster mushroom Pleurotus spp., and in Shitake Lentinus edodes. The bacterial brown blotch disease, caused by the bacterium P. tolaasii, has been one of the most serious bacterial diseases for the oyster mushroom. The disease often occurs over a large geographical area.The disease incidence has been different each year. Once the disease occurred on a farm, it became very difficult to control before all of the substrate bags were removed from the farm. Tolaasin, an extracellular lipodepsipeptide toxin produced by P. tolaasii, has proven to be the major virulence factor. When P. ostreatus develops the brown blotch symptom, it continues to rot due to a volatile toxin, tovsin, produced by P. tolaasii only when in contact with P. ostreatus.Preliminary data also indicates that P. ostreatus fruiting body components activate tolaasin production.It supports the hypothesis that P. tolaasii strains cause disease in P. ostreatus and have mechanisms that enable them to interact specifically with P. ostreatus.

The pathogen causes blotch symptoms on the pileus, forming membrane pores and disrupting the cellular membrane structure. The disease is characterized by the formation of brown lesions on mushroom caps and by bacterial growth in and discoloration of the stipes. These lesions consist of slightly concave spots, which can be round or spreading. Typically, spotting occurs at or near the edge of mushroom caps. Blotches occur when mushrooms remain wet for a period of h after watering, the brown spots and blotches enlarge and coalesce with others. The affected areas are sunken and covered with sticky material. However, the disease affects only the top external layers of the pileus tissues and is restricted to 2–3 mm below the pileus surface.Bacteria may reach and colonize on the surface of the pileus during the early fruiting body development stage while the young pileus is still in contact with the substrate. Greater bacterial population from spawned substrates may result in more severe infection. Disease incidence of primordia may result directly from the bacterial colonization from the substrate. Disease severity in the pileus is consistent with primordia disease incidence for tested strains with inoculation on spawned substrates. It is important to control the transfer of pathogen from the spawned substrate to the pileus during the early fruiting body development stages in order to manage this disease. Huge economic damage is due to a rapid spread of the bacterial pathogen in P. eryngii cultivations and effective biological or chemical control measures are scarce. In fact, some Pseudomonas isolates were screened for their antagonistic ability toward P. tolaasii; however their in vivo suppressive effect was not satisfactorily proven.Biological control methods with antagonistic microorganisms' and/or specific phages have also been investigated. Tsukamoto et al. reported that a gram-positive bacterium, strain 9045, detoxifies tolaasins produced by P.

tolaasii and significantly suppresses the onset of the disease in P. ostreatus. Another advantage of using strain 9405 is that it is saprophytic to P. ostreatus, in contrast to Pseudomonas fluorescens, which could be pathogenic to cultivated mushrooms by producing various antifungal agents and is closely related to P. tolaasii. According to Zhang et al, strain was resistant to brown blotch disease. However, it has rarely been cultivated by growers, because the fruiting bodies are very fragile and can easily be broken during harvest and transport.

Soft Rot

The genus Pantoea includes several species that are generally associated with plants, either as epiphytes or as pathogens. The gram-negative bacterium Pantoea spp. has been reported as a causal agent of soft rot disease with symptoms of water-soaked lesions on the stipes and pileus of P. eryngii. The typical symptoms of soft rot disease include a dark brown water drop in the early stages of infection, followed by the development of water-soaked lesions on the stipe and cap of mushrooms within 8 days after the mushrooms are transferred to the cultivation room. The lesions expand gradually and constitute a viscous, mucus-like fluid, finally leading to a mushy soft rot accompanied by an offensive odor during growth. Liu et al. isolated strains belonging to Pantoea beijingensis (growth occurs at 10–37 °C) from lesions on the fruiting body of P. eryngii exhibiting symptoms of water-soaked lesions and soft rot in the stipes and pilei. Compounds containing active chlorine are, at present, the most commonly utilized chemicals for bacterial disease control.Watering with concentrations at 175 ppm active chlorine were effective for the reduction of soft rot disease of P. eryngii without affecting mushroom yield.

Stipe Necrosis

Ewingella americana was identified as an opportunistic pathogen.Concerning Enterobacteriaceae, little is known about their prevalence and their contribution to the total microbial load of cultivated mushrooms. E. americana was identified as the causal agent of internal stipe necrosis on symptomatic samples collected from mushroom farms.Reyes et al. demonstrated the predominance of E. americana in biota of retail fresh P. ostreatus.The symptoms of internal stipe necrosis appear as a variable browning reaction in the center of the mushroom stipe.Examined in longitudinal section, the brown tissue extends from the base of the stalk to the cap, but rarely penetrates the cap tissue. Affected mushrooms may be wet in appearance, but frequently, at harvest; the brown tissue is dry and has completely collapsed, leaving a hollow center.In all cases, symptoms are visible only at harvest. The occurrence of internal stipe necrosis disease has occasionally been associated with water-logging of the mushroom stalks at an early development stage, and it is therefore important to maintain good evaporation from the bed surface at all times. In P. ostreatus, symptoms consisted of soft rot and mild browning of the tissues. According to González et al, E. americana is pathogenic in P. eryngii, although its presence was not dominant in the analyzed samples, being isolated in only 10% of them.However, Reyes et al. reported that the presence of this bacterium was high in commercial products. These results indicate that the pathogen is found in crops and increases during storage.

Lecanicillium fungicola is a devastating pathogen in the mushroom industry, which causes significant losses in the commercial production of Pleurotus spp. This mold causes dry bubble disease in commercially cultivated mushroom.Although its pathogenicity for other species has not been established, it has been isolated from numerous other basidiomycetes. On inoculation of healthy P. ostreatus, these isolates caused disease and could be reisolated. L. fungicola has also been mentioned as a pathogen of Pleurotus pulmonarius. However, L.

fungicola is not often found on wild mushroom, does not have a wide host range and might more often infect already decaying mushrooms.

Two distinct symptom syndromes are observed on the development stage of the sporophores at the time of infection. Infection of sporophores at the pin or button stage resulted in the development of typical dry bubbles, amorphous masses of sporophore tissue.In contrast, mature sporophores showed cracking and curling of the tissues and depressed, brown, necrotic areas.In advanced stages, a gray weft of mycelium and conidia frequently covered the surface of infected sporophores.The control of L. fungi cola relies on strict hygiene, regulation of the environment and the routine fungicide spray program. Few chemicals can be used for the control of dry bubble because the host is also sensitive to fungicides. Notably, the development of resistance of L. fungicola has been reported against the fungicides that are used to control dry bubble disease. The effective and currently legal chemical control for dry bubble disease is Sporgon (active ingredient: prochloraz-manganese). Sensitivity of L. fungicola to Sporgon has decreased, therefore increasing concentrations of Sporgon must be used to combat dry bubble disease. Another management technique that has been recently researched is the use of volatile 1-octen-3-ol on infected hosts of L. fungicola. While more research is needed to contribute its effects on management, it has been shown that 1-octen-3-ol inhibits the germination of L. fungicola and that enhanced levels can effectively control the pathogen.

Green Mold

The commercial production of oyster mushroom has been seriously affected by green mold epidemics. The causal agents of green mold disease of cultivated oyster mushroom are Trichoderma spp. (T. asperellum, T. atroviride, T. citrinoviride, T. hazianum, T. longibrachiatum, T. pleurotum, T. pleuroticola and T. virens).Trichoderma species are asexual, soil-inhabiting filamentous fungi with teleomorphs belonging to the genus Hypocrea (Ascomycota, Pyrenomycetes, Hypocreales, Hypocreaceae). Trichoderma pleurotum has been found only on cultivated P. ostreatus and its substrate.In contrast, Trichoderma pleuroticola has been found both on wild and cultivated P. ostreatus, as well as on the natural and productive substratum of the oyster mushroom. Trichoderma green mold infection in edible basidiomycetes has been known for a long time. The appearance of green fungal sporulation in oyster mushroom substrates are they typical green mold symptoms. In severe outbreaks, no mushrooms are produced from the contaminated substrates. Green mold infection of P. ostreatus is supposed to be transmitted by substrate for mushroom cultivation41. Woo have observed that Trichoderma species are present at the initial phase of substrate preparation, but later disappear with pasteurization. However, they can be found again in the substrate after inoculation with Pleurotus spp.(spawning), during spawn run (incubation phase) and in the harvesting cycles. The substrate is exposed to green mold infection mostly during spawn run, when the substrate temperature is increased up to 30 °C due to the generation of metabolic heat by mushroom mycelia, whereas no growth is observed at 15 °C. The optimal pH for Trichoderma spp. Growth is acidic-neutral conditions (pH 5–7). This information suggests that adjusting the pH of the substrate to might slow down the growth of Trichoderma spp., resulting in a decrease of infection spread. The mycelial growth of Trichoderma spp. is completely inhibited by pasteurization at 60 °C for 10 h. The mycelial growth of green mold occurred at its maximum in 80% of relative humidity conditions.Komoń-Zelazowska et al.Suggested the application of calcium hydroxide on the affected area.The hypothesis of a possible reduction of T. pleurotum infection by substrate alkalization may be further supported by the fact that

Pleurotus spp. Green mold is not reported to be a severe problem in the United States, where the addition of lime to increase pH to 7.5 is widely practiced. However, this treatment seems to be ineffective against T. pleuroticola.The use of fungicides benomyl, thiabendazole and prochloraz was also reported to be effective.Prochloraz was shown to be the most effective fungicide for the inhibition of mycelial growth in green molds, because the amount of resistant Trichoderma spp. isolates was the lowest when analyzing this fungicide. Prochloraz, benomyl and propineb were found to inhibit spore germination of benomyl-susceptible isolates in a proper way, while chlorothalonil was effective for benomyl-resistant strains. According to Hatvani, thymol, ferulic acid, (+)-menthol, and (−)-menthol inhibited green mold growth at concentrations as low as 0.08 mg ml to 1.25 mg ml.

Cobweb

Several species of Cladobotryum, including C. dendroides, C. mycophilum, C. varium, C. multiseptatum, and C. verticillatum are known to be the causal agents of "cobweb disease" in the cultivated mushroom Agaricus bisporus and are found in mushroom-growing countries worldwide. However, in 2009–2010, some commercially grown P. eryngii began to show similar symptoms to the fungal disease caused by Cladobotryum mycophilum in A. bisporus.The spores are relatively large and multicellular, being easily dislodged from the sporulating colony by external disturbances such as watering, air circulation systems, and harvesting9. Conidia were able to germinate and grow in 4 h. This fact suggests that the spores are very readily dispersed in the air and growth of conidia is an important causative factor of cobweb disease in P. eryngii. Air-borne spores from affected crops might contaminate reusable plastic bottles, substrates, and transportation systems, and the pathogen could rapidly spread from farm to farm.

This is the main mode of transmission by which the pathogen is distributed to mushroom farms.One of the main symptoms is a cobweb-like growth of fungal mycelium over the surface of the mushrooms. The colonies on the surface rapidly overwhelm the mushrooms and develop several spores within 3–4 days. The mycelium can quickly cover the king oyster mushroom debris, pin-heads, stalks, pileus and gills, eventually resulting in decomposition of the entire fruit body. The colonized surface turns pale brown or yellow, accompanied by cracking of the stipe surface. The fruit body eventually turns dark brown and becomes rancid, with an offensive odor. The fungal pathogen is sensitive to metrafenone (0.025 ppm), prochloraz manganese

(0.3 ppm), chlorothalonil (0.45 ppm), benomyl and carbendazim (<1.0 ppm) as well as moderately sensitive to thiophanate-methyl (2.0–8.0 ppm) and thiabendazole (4.85 ppm). To reduce this risk, benomyl and carbendazim should be used with caution only when mushroom growers know for certain that the pathogen they wish to control is sensitive to benzimidazole. In addition, combining the active ingredient with prochloraz manganese and thiophanate-methyl might help to prevent or at least decrease the risk of the pathogen becoming resistant.

Brown Spot

Gliocladium roseum Bainier were obtained from diseased P. eryngii. Symptoms consist of brow spot curling of the tissues, sometimes even shrinking, and cracking of the infected fruit bodies. The optimum temperature for conidial germination and mycelial growth of G. roseum is °C. It is also pathogenic to Pleurotus cystidosus and Pleurotus sajor-caju.

Viral diseases

Mycoviruses are widespread in fungi, including plant-pathogenic fungi. In most cases, they have been reported to be cryptic or show few symptoms leading to latent infection in host cells. Interestingly, the symptoms were observed throughout the culture when a certain mushroom spawn was inoculated58. Bacterial diseases such as brown blotch disease by P. tolaasii are generally restricted to a local area of culture. This led to the conclusion that the symptoms originate from virus-infected spawn. Mycoviral infection symptoms include retarded mycelia and fruiting body growth, fruiting body development inhibition, and malformations of the fruiting body40. In 1980, P. pulmonarius virus (Ppv) was isolated from mycelia and basidiocarps of P. pulmonarius47. P. eryngii Spherical Virus (PeSV) was isolated from P. eryngii mushroom, with severe epidemic symptoms. Transmission electron microscope showed that it was spherical with a 31-nm-diameter. Fruiting bodies of P. eryngii showed symptoms such as short and stout stems, and flattened caps with irregular shapes. The mycelia taken from the tissue of basidiocarp exhibited abnormally retarded growth on a solid medium. Curing of the viruses essentially eliminate the symptoms, indicating that they are the causative agents of the disease. Therefore, it is conceivable that many uncharacterized mushroom diseases may be related to mycoviral infection.

"La France" Disease

Ro et al. isolated the oyster mushroom isometric virus (OMIV). The characteristics of examined OMIV suggest that it is not related to known P. ostreatus-infecting viruses such as PoV1, which is a spherical virus that contains two dsRNA genomes and has a diameter of 30 nm. Typical symptoms of viral disease on oyster mushroom are quite similar to "La France" disease which is a well-known viral disease in A. bisporus, in which fruiting body formation delay, shortening in stipe, abnormal shape and thin mushroom caps are the major symptoms; fruiting bodies are not formed at all on some infected mushroom beds and viral-infected hyphae grow very slowly on agar and their density is very low.

Die-Back

Pleurotus spp. is generally cultivated under well-controlled environmental conditions, and its cultivation is thus largely free from diseases from external origin. However, mushroom industries often suffer from spawn-related diseases, most notably the die-back disease, which originates from a viral infection40. Yu et al.isolated the first single-stranded ssRNA mycovirus, named oyster mushroom spherical virus (OMSV), from a cultivated oyster mushroom, P. ostreatus. The authors detected the virus in all 102 samples collected from 102 different commercial farms with the epidemic. The symptoms are rather complex and the disease spreads fast. An outbreak of such disease in a commercial farm often leads to a complete loss of yield and it is difficult to control. OMSV was not detected in healthy mushrooms, and when OMSV from diseased mushrooms was cured, the epidemic disappeared. This strongly suggests that OMSV is a causative agent of the disease. Another P. ostreatus-infecting spherical dsRNA virus was discovered, being named. In contrast to OMSV, which is directly related to mushroom disease, infections by PoV1 did not show any distinct morphological or growth phenotypes.

Mice

The final pest of major importance to Thai mushroom cultivators is mice. Mice are most commonly a problem when cultivating mushrooms in plastic bags as they will eat the grain in the bags and, in so doing, remove a great deal of growing substrate and mushroom spawn from the bags. Mice might also eat immature mushrooms growing in the bags or destroy them while searching for grain. A potential problem with mice can be prevented by removing the grain substrate from the bags prior to beginning cultivation (this will have no effect on production) and by setting traps around the area of production. Poisons should not be used to kill mice as the mice might transfer the poison to the mushroom spawn, rendering the mushrooms inedible. Although there are several possible pest problems facing Thai mushroom cultivators, any farmer following good sanitation and pest prevention practices will be able to cultivate mushrooms with little fear of reduced yields due to pest infestation.

Molds

Molds are a common problem for mushrooms cultivated in plastic bags. The molds, usually green or black in color, are a result of temperature and humidity within the bag being higher than ambient conditions. Such molds are a common problem in plastic bags not yet opened for cultivation. Molds are usually first seen growing on the sorghum grain substrate near the plug end of the bag and, if left unchecked, moving down the sides of the bag completely covering and consuming the mushroom spawn. To prevent molds from emerging, prior to cultivation store the plastic bags in a place free from excessive heat or high humidity. If molds do emerge, separate the mold-infected bags from the non-infected bags, and use a knife or spoon to scrape away the mold, being careful to scrape away 1-2 cm of growing substrate below the mold to be sure all of the mold has been removed. Discard the mold and substrate and cultivate the mushrooms as usual, keeping the infected bag away from non-infected bags to ensure that the mold, if it reemerges, will not infect other bags of spawn. Because it will be impossible to remove mold entirely from a bag of spawn, the mold may continue to emerge and few, if any mushrooms will grow. Hence, if the mold reemerges after one attempt at removal, the bag should be discarded and replaced with a non-infected one to ensure that the mold will not spread to other bags and reduce mushroom production.

Insects

Insects are another pest that can significantly affect mushroom production.Ants and termites are the two main insect pests of mushrooms in Thailand. They can cause problems for farmers growing mushrooms in plastic bags, logs and beds by eating the growing substrate and, in some cases, the spawn, greatly reducing potential mushroom production. Insect problems are easily prevented by following good sanitation practices at the cultivation site. This is done by spreading lime on the ground at the site of production and/or spraying a mild pesticide (e.g., Malathion, Sevin-, Pyrethrum) over the same area before beginning cultivation. If cultivating in a mushroom house, a 30-60 cm band of soil surrounding the outside of the house, as well as all the ground surface area within the house, should be limed and/or sprayed. This will kill all the insects that might be living in the soil and prevent others from entering from untreated areas.Cultivation of mushrooms can begin one week after the initial treatment. Therefore, the perimeter around the house can be retreated every 15-30 days to ensure that insect pests cannot enter. (Note: Most people will not encounter any major insect problems while cultivating mushrooms. Therefore, it is best to grow mushrooms at the site at least once before engaging in a pesticide program in order to establish whether spraying is actually necessary. Do not encourage pesticide use by farmers with limited experience in growing mushrooms.) If insect pests have infested the production site extensively, they may cause great damage to the mushroom crop and should be eradicated. If the insects are infesting mushrooms being grown in plastic bags, all the mushrooms should be collected from the bags, then the outside of the bags should be sprayed with a very mild pesticide (e.g., Malathion, Sevin-, Pyrethrum). Be careful not to allow the pesticide to come in contact with the spore inside the bags! After all insects are eradicated or have left the area (usually in 1-2 days), water the bags generously with clean water in order to flush away any pesticide residue left on the bags. Wait 10-15 days before harvesting any mushrooms for consumption. Do not eat any mushrooms that may have emerged immediately following the pesticide application. (Note: Insect infestation will not usually warrant the use of pesticides.Use pesticides only in the most severe cases and be very careful in their application-especially with regard to mushroom harvest and consumption.)

Conclusion

It promises to supply food with good quality protein produced from worthless lignocellulosic wastes of varied origins. In future, newer mushrooms are likely to be added to diversify the portfolio of the cultivated mushrooms and the production of the presently consumed mushrooms will increase with the genetic improvement of the strains and the advancements in the cultivation technology.